Idle Fragments

Donna Edwards

Idle Fragments

Acknowledgements

Thank you to my family and friends for listening without judgement and for your ongoing encouragement. Who said that only poets love poetry?

Special thanks to:
Wayne my husband for his tireless critiquing
Brett and Dylan my sons for their perseverance
Tom Anderson for suggesting the Edge Festival
and for sharing with his class
Rocco Fazzari for amazing cover art
Sonya Caddy for fearless editing
Stephen Matthews and team for believing in me

Excerpts from
'The Silky Veils of Ardor' by Joni Mitchell 1977
'Dulce et Decorum est' by Wilfred Owen 1920
'Dream Stuff' by David Malouf 2000
Benoit Mandelbrot 1979
Peter Goers ABC Radio 891
'Hot Rod Lincoln' by Charlie Ryan 1955
'Barbarian Days' by William Finnegan 2015
'Pale Blue Dot' by Carl Sagan 1994

For the love in my life

Idle Fragments
ISBN 978 1 76041 535 8
Copyright © text Donna Edwards 2018
Cover: Rocco Fazzari, *Harbour Beach*, 2016

First published 2018 by
GINNINDERRA PRESS
PO Box 3461 Port Adelaide 5015
www.ginninderrapress.com.au

Contents

Preface	9
Global Nonsense	**11**
Time Will Tell	13
Who Would Have Guessed	15
Where Are Our Warriors	16
I Think Not	17
South African Blues	18
Beyond the Pale	19
Miracles Required	21
In Omnibus Caritas	22
Haiku Horror	23
How Can We Celebrate	24
Farewell Money	25
Terror Time	26
Strawberries and Poppies	27
What a Year	29
In a Perfect Storm	30
What a Nuisance	31
Careful What You Wish For	32
So Naive	33
Flee Refugee	34
Closer to Home	**35**
Four Seasons in Adelaide	37
One Season in Wales	38
Once a Decade	39
Once a Year	40
Good Morning	41
Vacancy	42
Fogbow	43

Watch and Learn	44
Thirty-six Degrees	45
Rocco and the Cabbage Moth	46
Arrival of the Species	47
Boring Days	48
Could've Been a Costly Argument	49
Los Ruinas	51
The Dirty ½ Dozen	52
Farewell	54
The Second Pack Down	56
Off in Peace	57

Who Are These People — 59

Sad About Geoffrey	61
Where Art Thou	62
To be Continued	63
The Incident	64
Wounded Angels	66
Lost for Words	67
Moleskins and Wax	68
Reticent Resonance	69
Breaking Broccoli	70
Well Beyond the Game	72
Sixty-one	73
Stubborn	75
MiL and the Mutt	76
The Order of Things	77
Who Are You Tonight	79
The Sixtieth	80
Boxing Day	81

Things Get Personal — 83

My Jewellery Box	85

The Brooch	86
The Waiting Game	87
The Ceremony	90
The Butterfly	92
Fade Away	94
Time on My Hands	95
Nana's Gift	96
Chemical Fragility	97
I Don't Buy It	98
Where Will It End	100
The Proximity of Things	102
No Time to Waste	103
Cubanism	104
The Grumball	106
Mother and Son	107
Finding Fontaine	108
What Now	**109**
Who Are These People	111
The Coming Out	112
Three Months Later	113
Roads Too Travelled	**117**
I Want to be a Wallaby	119
I See the Light	120
Forty in the Shade	121
You're Kidding Me	122
I'm Flying Along	123
It Was the Winter	124
Brecon Beacon	125
Where Devils Venture	126
It's a Sad Thing	127
Sweet Infant	128

Everyone Loved Jack	129
Not the Way to Go	130
A Final Word	**133**
My Little Universe	135
About the Author	136

Preface

Idle Fragments is about waiting and watching, introspection and reflection. It is a selection of poems about life with all the nuances of being human at a global, local and personal level.

Idle Fragments may have you wondering if the world has gone completely mad as we just idle around letting it pass. Everyday observations are laid to word in stark reality, sometimes tenderness and often humour.

Whether you have time on your hands or not a second to waste, perhaps we long to be idle in our own fragmented way.

Global Nonsense

Time Will Tell

Brexit was trumped
Some ponder
Has the world gone completely mad
What more can I write amongst an avalanche of global commentary

It was only a matter of time
Not if but when
So educated
So connected
So few with so much
So many with so little
So many guns in
So many hands

Is irony on steroids
Desperate millions electing a billionaire

Yet again
A protest about the System
The Establishment
Democracy
But what alternatives
Dictatorship
Perhaps communism
Fascism
Socialism
Feudalism
Why not a monarch for all

Or let's try
Fundamentalism
Monasticism
Fanaticism
Why not a despot for all

None of the above
The people have voted

Make it Great
Let them eat cake
Sprinkle it with ice

Yet again
The Minders
Will be in overdrive
Let them have nox
Sprinkle it with rocket fuel

Who Would Have Guessed

Not Martha's vineyard
Caught withering on the vine
Ripe for the crushing

Where Are Our Warriors

What has happened to us
Are we so swamped in this deluge of distraction
Unrecognisable Australia
Once a melting pot of multiculturalism
Celebrating diversity
Patriotic
Welcoming
After decades of whiteness
Have we returned to
Nauseating nationalism
Disguised as eloquent elitism
Stealth like
Shifting across classlessness
Towards bogan bullying
Sadly the old race card rears its vile head yet again
Driving a wedge through our humanity
Who shall we let in
Who shall we leave out
So popular
So compelling

Why does no one roar with disapproval

As we bid farewell to our strong and fearless bureaucracy
The institutions that served to steer our nation
Gutted by short-sighted politicians
Feathered by favoured media
While we watch and whisper
Who will fight our battles
Let's just post on fake book and choose a cruise
Twits…all of us

I Think Not

Why do I have no inspiration and enchanted words of love
Brimming with life
Delightful as a Shakespeare sonnet
Tender as Keats
As tearful as Blake
Perhaps romantic Eliot
Or Dante's awe
And Thoreau's nature

If they were alive now
Would they be immune or smothered too by this deluge
Such brittle shards of unkindness scattered across our globe
Would they bristle as we do
Raising quill against callousness and cruelty
Could they still whisper sweet wonders
Their light shining through

Hope fades

South African Blues

Townships of hardship
A deep financial divide
The new apartheid

Beyond the Pale

The Centre Left just scraped in
But the Far Right nailed it
Frightening votes and hopes for Austria once again
Reject austerity
Reject economic reform
Reject refugees

While not far off referendum resignations
Are now quite common
England of course
Then Italy
Such a humiliating loss
Ciao-style political chaos
Fascists feared
Reject the lot

While we're at it let's dump the Euro
So nerve wracking
Big bonds
Spiralling debt
And all that
Who wants competitiveness anyway

Heading for the poll
Another round of rancour
England
France
Netherlands
Germany
Italy
Want to be elected
Refuse to be rejected
Populism must prevail

On the back of Brexit let alone Trump
Oh the unpredictability of neo-geo-politico cheerio
What volatility serious instability
Let's not mention all that tension
From the waking giant
And keep a watch on that Putin mob
Meanwhile out there in the boondocks a pure bombshell
Key resignation
The top of his game

What next
An absence of malice
Unlikely
The media is on to it
Long live populism

Yes my friends
It's all happening
On that pale blue dot

Miracles Required

Thank Mohamed for Islam
It makes millions if not billions of people subdued and peaceful
Let's transform the fraction of fundamentalists who ruin that peace
While we're at it why not eliminate poverty

In Omnibus Caritas

The economists got it right
And most agree
There is no utopia
Just an unstoppable struggle
For an unreachable equilibrium
In a multilevel degenerate state of chaos
Allowing no evolution without mutation
Order and disruption everywhere

Interstellar enormity
Galaxies collide
Universal expansion
Global domination
International nuances
National boundaries
State skirmishes
Local jurisdiction
Community disputation
Family feuds
Individual inequity
Internal indigestion
Microscopic malice

So let's just get on with it
We could even try politeness
Could you imagine a polite mess
While we're at it
Perhaps a semblance of clarity
Even a touch of charity

Haiku Horror

Savage Aleppo
Millions flee persecution
Thousands are too late

How Can We Celebrate

Sixty-two people own the same wealth as the bottom
three point six billion people
Yes
You heard me right
According to Oxfam December twenty sixteen
And here I am waiting for dividends
So I can buy everything needed for a
Jolly good celebration
I wonder how those sixty-two manage to manage their parties
I wonder how the other billions manage

Farewell Money

Forty years of labouring
Selling our only resource
We ought to have spoken up sooner for the new breed
Those poor souls on contract
Barely making ends meet from week to week
Not knowing if a job would last
Overtime long gone and don't mention the union
But those who spoke up were not seen again
Restructured
Made redundant

Some called it f*#k you money
Polite ones said goodbye money
Any way you looked
It was cashed-up courage just before retirement
With unmitigated freedom to state the obvious
We only needed a fair go

Some leaders think that workers are revolting
We reject that sentiment
But is it any wonder

Terror Time

It's London this time
Poor lost souls yet so relieved
Our loved ones unharmed

Strawberries and Poppies

I picked a poppy in honour of my father
A strapping navy man HMAS *Murchison*
Poisoned by radiation
That slow silent assassin long after Montebello
Another casualty of war yet not technically a statistic amongst the millions before

Pressed carefully so delicate inside that latest spy novel
Nestled deep in my backpack
Well travelled it was
Picked from a steep cliff near a cave where people once lived
And men fought for centuries over that strategic ground
It would be smuggled across borders
Destination top shelf Australia in the Korean War Volume 2 Combat Operations
I bow before that UK Customs sign
Abandoned on some random seat inside a brochure about a beautiful Marrakech garden
I had no heart for a litter bin

My silent prayer floats away
Perhaps my poppy will be discovered by another
Honoured in their book
A beautiful lonely flower

What was I thinking it was just bluff
No customs inspector or hard-pressed poppy police

My travel over I relax eating a ripe strawberry
I wonder about my sacrificial poppy
Its journey incomplete
Plucked in its prime
I ponder about the millions who fought to set us free
We can wander and wonder
Free to grow strawberries in peace
With the freedom to savour that most delicious fruit

I think about my father
His brother the toughened sergeant
My son the army lieutenant
His friend the air force pilot
Street and bikie gangs
Children soldiers
Now ISIS
Such different degrees of tantalising promises

For our fallen and serving disrespectful comparison is unintended
Yet my mind returns to that long gone war poet
Strawberries and poppies
Blood and bravery
Sweet and honourable
Wilfred Owen's 'old lie' continues its arduous journey
And recruitment honesty is still absent on most fronts

What a Year

We cried purple rain in stardust during reports that
Santa blew up an Istanbul nightclub

All of us
Speechless as a Nobel poet
Caught shaking his head

Meanwhile
Like poor lost souls on a sinking ship
Millions flee poverty to fenced off wealth

Closer to home some random lets off a firecracker
And all hell breaks loose

Why am I relieved to hear that Santa's behind bars

In a Perfect Storm

We hold hands with global partners
An abandoned car industry stalks as
Mining collapses
Commodities correct
And pretty property bubbles burst all around us
Construction peaks
While AAA is lost on the path

Once robust
Banks go bust
Then of course
China slows down
Trump factors in
On top of European disintegration
Brexit Frexit and Grexit

What's left
A dirty sand pit in a discarded rusty playground
But there's never been a better time to transition
To the new economy
Jobs galore
What's in store
Retail
Tourism
Health

Was Henny Penny a prophet
Not my idea of a pretty crystal ball

What a Nuisance

We call them boat people
Captained by people smugglers
On leaky vessels not fit for scrap
Faced with a five year process
Now that's determination
All legitimate refugees
Of course
Well funded terrorists fly in

Why not toss them overboard
So well provisioned
Pretty orange life pod rafts
Current of the day
Indonesia

Let's lock them up
Throw away the key
Better still
Strike a deal
Our Government
Hell-bent on human trafficking
Has mastered the art
Nauru to America
Now that's all heart

Say not a word
It's an operational matter
You're just the taxpayer
And it's none of your business
Yet are we not all boat people
Don't ask such stupid questions
Leave that for *Q&A*

Careful What You Wish For

My father could tell captivating yarns around our dinner table yet never spoke of war
Again we begged wanting stories…snippets for fright night
He weakened
Five wide-eyed young faces watched as he glazed over drawn into secret compartments
Regretting our pestering for in those moments we peered deep into his soul and should not have been there

How I marvel at human imagination…minds power
For those words seared an image so vivid though I was never there hidden for safer processing decades later

Creeping through stifling jungle
No time for earths exquisiteness
Lost conscripts of fear
Rifle ready
Their mate displayed in unspeakable savagery
Intended to unnerve shock demoralise anger
Swallow your horror soldier

His telling ended
No one spoke
I prayed that soldier's mother never knew
A part of me wants to transfer oral history to share his cautionary tale
Perhaps secretly you want to know…can it compete with Hollywood gore

How can we turn another cheek when all faith in humanity is lost
This raw sordid truth shall go to my grave

So Naive

Tandem footprints and bird prints
Little parallel universes on that pristine beach
Optimism beckons anew
Beauty in coexistence
Perhaps we can do it

Yet pessimism stalks with breathless disappointment
As weeds strangle saplings
For are we not the creators of our great Pacific garbage patch
A veritable trash vortex

Slow learners we are

Flee Refugee

…and he wrote in sand
Farewell my beautiful beach
Taken by the sea

Closer to Home

Four Seasons in Adelaide

Spring is here
With birds and bees
And blossom on the almond trees

Summer arrives
On the run
So much sand surf and sun

Autumn falls
Bright with colour
Fine cirrus cloud like no other

Winter stalks
With such abandon
…leave town

One Season in Wales

Summer arrives
In total confusion
Flee to the equator

Once a Decade

Keen to take whiff
Cultivation for a nation
And raising funds to save that Sumatran Titan Arum
So here we are lining up to smell a corpse flower
Blooming hell
Beautifully disturbing

Once a Year

With regular hilarity
We prance in flags
The bay our playground
Joy girls on paddleboards
Young enough to laugh
Old enough not to care
Crazy wild all of us

Into the warm night
Sweet banter goes on
Faces raised to stars
That southern cross in its glory
As our men cook up a catch
Advancing our cause

And the shape of the day
so exquisite once again

Good Morning

Row after row
Page after page
So vibrant
Smart
Decisions decisions
Finger poised
Now which app to choose

Vacancy

They called her
The Pit Bull in Lipstick
Delighting in glee
As she watched
Grown men cry
Far worse treatment for women

So deserving of that voodoo doll
Made from a toilet roll

The Machine was impressed
Right down their alley
Strategy and tactics in one nasty shape
Suck them dry
Spit them out
Two maybe three years maximum
Captured in mortgage
The bigger the better
Let's finish them off with a placebo
Some exit interview

The Machine goes on
As does that piece of work

Fogbow

Chittering wakes me
Well before sunrise
So comfortable
Our great southern ocean
Pounds away with no concern for anyone
As sunlight warms the space
Shades of green remind me
Where I am

Sunglasses found
I zip my way to fresh air
Lenses opaque as they hit the crisp
Clarity requires removal

What is this
My eyes deceive for a nanosecond
Fog so dense it triggers a childhood memory
I can hear my mother's voice
'Thick as pea soup'
Always a matter of fact she was

It is worthy of a deep slow breath
Hauntingly beautiful
I slow pirouette
Nature's delight
With a sweet surprise
Devoid of spectrum
A full rainbow in the mist

Watch and Learn

I recall bird prints only
In a vast pristine paradise
Belonging to endangered hooded plovers
Nesting on that isolated beach
Eggs in little scrapes on sand

I also see
Deep tire ruts beyond the NO VEHICLES sign
Garbage left untied
Bones and skins off fruit
Chip packets and plastic plates
Tissues in the breeze
Papers floating off
A pathetic party had

Disrespectful aftermath not yet done
For sadly I see
Little scrapes on sand
'I love you mum & dad'

Thirty-six Degrees

Waves pound across Cactus reef
That wild isolated shoreline
My faded yellow umbrella spreads wide enough
Lazily on its side a sun setting in sand
It's held down by a rock
Defying a raging northerly

In stark contrast
She's reading a Norwegian whodunnit set in frozen ice
Cooled by words
Blissful

But ignore March flies at your peril
Speed swat vital unless one is smothered
Apparently 'The Locals' Sandfly and Mozzie Stuff' works wonders
A pile mounts
Testament to constant vigilance a keen sense of touch and lightening reflex after years of practice

Not quite for the faint-hearted but it beats forty-five in the tent

Rocco and the Cabbage Moth

Same school different journey
Goers would say 'best education money couldn't buy'
He the famous artist
She the unknown poet
Shall I ask
It was the Class of '75
He is top row toward the right
She is sitting left of centre
He would go to art class
And bring back amazing pictures
She would go to home economics
And boil an egg
Both had fabulous lives
Of course
Australian Baby Boomers
He uses a variety of mediums
Even iPad sketch
She uses scraps of paper
Sometimes napkins
Decision made
Just ask him
But it's Sydney
He's probably sitting in traffic
Juggling a million rock oysters
She's pruning a rose in Adelaide
Perhaps next year
Hope flutters
Like an erratic little cabbage moth

Arrival of the Species

It's a stinker
Sitting behind net
Just minding my own business
Countless blighters battle to break in

Not while I'm cooking
My silent threat

Swatter at the ready
Lightning reflex and sharp retreat

Regret follows
Recalling radio talkback
Twelve hundred new species
Found across Australia
Mainly Coleoptera
Lepidoptera and Odnata
It's bug heaven

Poor thing
It could have been twelve hundred and one

Boring Days

He's reading
Barbarian Days
A Surfing Life
Bestseller
She's writing
'Boring Days
A surfing wife'
Unpublished
Surfers anticipate and congregate
Wives isolate and contemplate

Of course
We all have other interests
Surfers fish drink and drink
Wives cook clean and read
Most need a drink
Some surfers are handy
Around the houses they built
Waxing boards
Making sinkers
Tying knots
Brewing and bottling
Stoking outside fires
Getting ready for mates

Could've Been a *Costly Argument*

There was musing at the station for word had gone around
It was arsenic!
Holy wine-stained moleskins
Five minutes before the race
He must have eaten a pine post
Our vet at his best

Scandal on the West Coast
Not *Alert the World*
As rotten as *Fine Cotton*
Perhaps it's just the lace
That horse as mad as a fascinator
Oh gosh
What will the fashionistas say

Why not blame the mouse plague
Dusted spiked
In grain
Wrong place
Wrong time

Grazing
It could've been around that old cattle dip
He was seen
Quite the mystery and anyone's guess

That jockey was in order
Correct weight
And which horse was pipped at the post
Hold onto your horses
All bets are off

It might have been a jab
Let's blame it on the TAB
Such big stakes

Never before a stranger strainer
An innocent bystander I say
What if anything did the vice president know

Keep your Akubra on
He'll keep us posted

Los Ruinas

From the ruins
Each stone seen
Chosen and screened
Selected with precision
Little indecision
Planned in his mind
Discerning
Artistic
Chipping away
Rising cautiously on that cliff

Rooms evolve
One wall at a time
Corners linger
A fireplace unfolds
Beckoning embers
Awaiting icy winters
Roof conceals that expansive blue sky
Sea views glazed over
Chunky timber decks expand in welcome compensation
Inviting culinary delight the wood oven
Stands above laboured pavers
Guest room complete
Studio replete
The lintel is chiselled
A♥S
In it together
Her hard earned cash
His back breaking labour
Stone walls continue through life's journey
Master and partner
Works of art

The Dirty ½ Dozen

Swarming like flies at a hint of surf
Roaming across sand tracks
A fish-casting snake-spotting gang of six
Pampered pooches I say
Cryovac meals prepared in advance
So worth the price
Their women free from men and mozzies
Perhaps a week or two

Half a dozen well educated clean-cut saintly boys
Minus that Good man
Fine wine
German beer
All the latest camping gear
So not ready for repairs
So ready for easy decline

They get on well except when there's swell
Star-studded nights
Raucous laughter
Washed out happy hours
Mallee root flames
Aahh
Stuffing their heads with leavened breads
Wind-blown days
Nothing really matters

Now with Ewok faces
Gazing at fire light
Scratching at midgee bite
Blowies galore
Hangovers to ignore
What more can one want?

Contented sighs all round
Cactus delivers without a crowd

Farewell

Hark
I hear a pack down
Each of us gaze
Through fly wire
A discrete distance
Patiently sipping
It's riveted restraint
No one ventures too soon
Cactus etiquette and all that
There's a straggler now
That's our cue
Top up coffee
Hats on

Strolling at just the right pace
A disinterested expression
Must not make an impression
The gathering takes shape
Coming from far and wide
Even a dog came for the ride
Rob to the power of two
Except one was injured from too much surf
No sympathy of course
Being the centre of attention
Just increased the tension
Which we all relished

It was a SWIFT camper van
We call for a permanent marker
Pre-text NOT required
They continue work ignored by all
It turns into a photo shoot

Then suddenly
Five reversing supervisors
Confusions reign
He shows no pain
Unlike the bumper

Such audacity
He tries to scare us
With a cockroach plague
No one leaves
Waves all round

See you later that was fun
Funniest pack down under the sun
We all disperse and watch the surf
Satisfied with a heckling well done

The Second Pack Down

We came
We heckled
They loved it
They left

Off in Peace

I can barely hear them
Men chatting
Metal clanging
Bolt upright
Oh no
We're missing a pack down

Recovery takes shape
He's leaving at three-thirty
We suspect a lie
How irritating having to do pack down math
First leg before roo-time
Now it's anyone's guess

We all wave from a distance and he is smiling

Who Are These People

Sad About Geoffrey

A repertoire so staggering
Yet diminished by his sheer interpretation
Giving thought existence in another form

Silenced in delight as they listen to one pianist
Australia's musical gift of artistic perfection
A constant composer
At three he twinkled Appassionata Sonata
Tozer sparkles in laughter

Well beyond prodigy
He toured the world
In Europe and China honoured as living treasure
Yet overlooked by our own

Where did he go
Was he born to play forced to work
A recluse in oblivion
Could he find meaning without applause

Why was he not our national living treasure

Where Art Thou

Mandelbrot
With your simple rules and complex patterns
Elaborate with infinitely complicated boundaries
Such is art of roughness and physical phenomena
Wispy cirrus and gigantic nimbus
Clouds of sand under pounding waves
Creating delicate lace pattern foam
Uncontrolled elemental sculpture
Discarding the unnecessary
With ever finer detail at increasing magnification
Tsunami to a ripple
Smaller versions of similar shape
Forests and trees and saplings
Sameness applies on whole not just its parts
Raindrops and deluge
Repetition everywhere
Grains of sand and shifting dunes
Idle fragments perfectly replicated
Rocks from mountains
Trickles to rivers
Molecular to interstellar
Ancestors toward future generations
Julia sets to join the case
Defined and chaotic
In their minds a plan of mathematical perfection

To be Continued

We opened our eyes
Hardly there
So unaware
Sensing not knowing
Connecting vague dots
Slowly piecing it together
Tears form words
Talk becomes speech
Walking then running
Discovery goes wild
We were bright stars
in our own universe back then
Facts stacked while dreams danced on
Truths dawn gradual
And time proceeds
Relentless labouring for shelter then lifestyle
Worlds collide and collude
Ourselves larger than life
But so diminished in its composition
Yet we laugh
Life and loves joyous crescendo
Random cells divide
They open their eyes
Hardly there
So unaware

The Incident

Who are these people
Security got the lot
About thirty bald head blue shirt
Another iced boxer
'Of course I'll press charges
Get that animal off the streets'
Police divulge an Incident Number
They suggest Victims of Crime
Awoken, she speeds to the aftermath
'Sup Bro'
'What sort of doctor says that' laments girlfriend

Mother
Glad he's alive refrains from comment
Father shakes his head
We gather around the coffin
I wish Popa could comment
Nana has no idea
Catching on much later loses three hours sleep
Uncle smirks
He's been there done that
Ditto for my cousin
Birthday Boy gets a tongue lashing from Mother
In the dog house once again
He extracts sympathy from his wing man

'You think it's funny' rings in my ears
Lip smashed I go down onto stainless
I get up

What was I thinking
Knocked once again hitting the urinal
Lucky it's flexible
My last thought

Four hours in emergency
Five stitches later
Jaw feels broken

Perhaps I'll give next weekend a rest

Wounded Angels

So sad
Two beautiful Angels
On separate paths
Tender scars
Wings now clipped
Yet still beautiful Angels
Time will see you fly again

Lost for Words

With deliberation
He says
I adore you
He takes my hand and
looks at me
Making certain I hear
And understand
He says it again

Speechless
Never before had words evoked such emotion
I believed him and it felt wonderful

I open my eyes
Thinking
It was all a dream
He thought it cute
Wanted the credit
'That was no dream
I was whispering in your ear last night'

Reality dawns through the Silky Veils of Ardor
I long to soar once more in my dream

Instead I'm thinking Mister Sandman
Has an irritating sense of humour

Moleskins and Wax

From entirely different backgrounds
They stood their ground
Near Korner store
While the town pub loomed bored

He wandered along that station track four decades ago
A townie in search of work
Waves down a gravelled road
That farmer crushed his clean hand in calloused dust
His son looked on thinking 'get a grip'

Hard work hard play
Amazing surf along the way
The perfect combine

Now leaning on the farmer's ute
His trusty sheep dog itching to go
Both their fathers now passed
All their children grown
Chewing the fat over nothing much
And silence sits like an old friend
They scheme a way to get together again

Reticent Resonance

He burnt us all a music mix
Back in two thousand and three
They danced to the beat
Dark glasses and tea towels on their head
Relishing attention
We laughed out loud

How melody stirs emotion
Those days have passed
A mateship severed
By god knows what
We wonder why
And wished it not

The other is fishing alone
Wearing a practical hat
Staring through a bird on the wing
Perhaps they've moved on
Why can't we

Breaking Broccoli

Observed without notice
'What a clever idea
Would you be so kind
It's such a struggle'

He was breaking bad
Just retrenched
Money stretched
Gripped tight he coughs out loud as camouflage
Ever so grateful she walks off smiling
He smirks and watches her go
His good deed done for the day

Guilt creeps up
Like humidity in a sauna that's way too hot
Lingering
Stifling
Is it against the law
Is it similar to removing lettuce leaves
Is there a supermarket breaking-broccoli inspector
He snatches a quick glance
What to do
Panic rises
With stealth precision
That stalk was laid bare on a can of beans
He smirks again perhaps crime does pay
Ten cents worth his guess
What next
Sultanas from fruit loaf

Above a giant pile of carrots a sign now reads
'Broccoli $2.99/kg
Please do not break off stem
Price is for whole'

No good deed goes unpunished

Well Beyond the Game

We search for each man
Fourth row down third from right
G Downey compelled to write
Third row down second from right
R Edwards sadly departed

Team mates or rivals
It matters not
Both men were dropped avoiding sweet victory
In that grand final
Our family amazed
As we gaze at the old black and white
West Torrens Football Club 1953
United by the team

Six decades gone
Never since seen
And each of us moved
By such a simple honourable gesture

Sixty-one

I look down
It feels different
How interesting
Where did it come from
Quite moist but firm
Smells sweet
Yuk
I won't eat that
It sticks to my fingers
Dark streaks on white poles
I admire my work
Quite the artist
Oh oh
My mother is yelling again

She stops
A strange laugh
Oh oh
Here it comes again
Oh the humiliation
Oh the shame
Where is my paper bag?
It's not so interesting now
So different the interpretation
Something about a Chiko roll
Smothered hands and face
Cot-rungs streaked brown
Poo Choo

Fifteen torturous years of it
Often in a crowded room
Fits of laughter

I just took it
My brother smirked
I always got him back
Sixty-one years later
The demented truth revealed
My brother did it!
I smirk and think to myself
Here…have a hunch and hand him the paper bag

But alas
I suspect he will only have to wear it once or twice

Stubborn

Thirty-seven years later
I open the lid for her
She takes the spoon
Stares a while
Hesitant
'It smells nice'
Cautious taste test
'What do you think?'
Another spoonful
No answer
Another spoonful
Then another
Intense concentration
It looks like she's enjoying it
Another spoonful
Then another
Non-stop
She scrapes the bottom
Finished
She licks her lips and smiles
Now her words are but a distant memory
'I don't like yogurt it tastes like Agarol'

MiL and the Mutt

That was our code
We could giggle about their antics
No one would know

Most wished for hot summer days
But that would cause dread
Anything over 30 degrees
And it was on
A house full of fur
His mother and her dog hunkered down
A week or more

Glued to the weather channel
She's praying for respite
Finally that thermometer drops
They leave
Vacuum working overtime

Sadly Mutt fell off the perch
But summer is on its way
So is MiL
They hope for a cool one

Now dear MiL has just passed in the depths of winter
No fiery brimstone awaits
And we yearn for just one more heatwave

The Order of Things

Crack
It was green
Too late he laments as it explodes onto seven below
Absolutely putrid
A mad dash across bitumen
More fertiliser

Everyone had their say
'You should have bought caged eggs'
'It probably hid for weeks'
'Never buy free range'
'Get your own chooks'
'Now everyone's an expert'
Grinning at his sad pun

A lone sweet voice pipes up
'Nature's layers should range free'

What was she thinking
The battle begins
'Whether it's 1,500 or 10,000 to a hectare
They are absolutely petrified to go outside
I can just hear those chooks now'
It's hell out there
Food and water in here
Predators everywhere
I'm staying right here thank you very much
Give me a cage any day
'Free range all right
Who wants to pick up eggs in that mess $500 a dozen' I say

'Dominate or die
They sort out the order
Peck each other to the death
Unless total submission'

She tries again
'But isn't that the way in nature. Freedom'

He's thinking she's in media infested La La Land
'Yet haven't you been vaccinated
So are those leather boots you're wearing my dear
And why don't you live in a cave'
His diatribe continues
'Billions get affordable protein'

He's lost her
Hands over ears closed eyes 'I'm not buying caged eggs'

Pecking order not yet sorted

Who Are You Tonight

Goldie Lochs and the three kids surfer business owner
And you
Victorian only two kids this time
Shall we take wine
It's a barbie let's not

That was fun
I think they believed us
Laughing about it later in their fancy RV

That was fun
I think they think we believed them
Laughing about it later in the old camper trailer

No one cared
No one dared

The Sixtieth

He stood tall
Axe in hand
Furry shoulders
A crazy hybrid – Goldilocks needs a hairdresser meets Hagar with anorexia

Surrounded by viscous pirates he showed no fear
His filthiest of Norsemen at the ready

A feast was served
Ale on tap
Slabs of meat
Rustic tarts

That Viking spawned pirates
So they gave him hell through raucous laughter
Then Happy Birthday bellowed
And vikings ate pavlova
As drunken pirates guzzled

Let the battle begin
A rowdy lot all of them

Boxing Day

The day was completely saturated
Even the dish sponge was wet before I started
Somewhere it's drought

We collapsed
Quite the Christmas
And what a year it's been
Facebook has no idea

Breathing deeply
Oblivious to waiting coffee
Even clean shaven
He deserves a kiss

Snoring at his feet
Oblivious to waiting rabbits
Sweet little Charlie
He deserves a bath

Things Get Personal

My Jewellery Box

He made me a jewellery box
Exquisite
Soft red velvet lined
Multi-tiered
Top lid and three drawers
Rich dark timber
Little gold knobs

Never before gifted such handcrafted beauty
My trinkets dishonour
Over time I nestled more worthy jewels in its care
Thinking of him with each opening and closure

Now we say farewell to a ray of sunshine
And I gaze on my jewellery box differently now
I see his experienced mind designing its shape
I see a diligent man choosing fine fabric
I see his beautiful face inspecting its surface
I see his strong hardworking hands perfecting its smoothness
I see his loving arms holding our sons
I see Ray

The Brooch

Grade One
An excited new recruit
I made my mother a brooch
Inside a pure white cockle shell
Collected by that inspired teacher
We pour plaster
Embed a safety pin
Finally dry
Ready for my design
Black stripes
She loves magpies
Gift wrapped in a finger painting
Of course

Over the years
With nothing better to do
I'd sneak a peek
First drawer down
Tucked safely next to beautiful lace handkerchiefs
My first work of art
Never to discard

Absent during her passing and sad clear out
I wonder where it journeyed
Longing for its placement in my fine red velvet
Deserving to be honoured
Sometimes I think about her smile wearing that brooch
A delicate lace handkerchief for my tears

The Waiting Game

Our swing was squeaky
Sunshine warming my face
Eyes shut tight to see colours
It took a while to understand a din in the distance
Recess and lunch breaks
Schoolyard clatter just down our street

It beckoned
I couldn't wait
July intake
Wrapped in a red wool coat
Pretty white collar
Black polished shoes
She talked to another Mother
While we smiled at each other
Bye

Holidays loomed
A prison sentence
Lacking class structure
Friends scarce
I named them Lazy Daisy Chain Days
In the back paddock
Cloud dreaming
So bored I could scream
With regular monotony ringing in my ears
'Good things come to those who wait'
Why do they say that

Later there were siblings galore
Dogs cats birds chickens
Fruit trees to choose
Our street full of kids

We played till nightfall
Then came teenage torture
How does anyone make sense of it
Irritating universal truths coexisting with shared pearls of wisdom
I couldn't wait to grow up
Grown-ups had all the fun
I couldn't wait to get a job
That meant money
Freedom

No one will take me serious
Economics
That will do
It paid off in the end
My life would really start

We had it all
Too much haste makes waste
But you haven't got a second to lose
Where is the wisdom in all of this
Random situational applicability called for
Yet skilfully avoided

Retirement is where it's at
So looking forward to grandchildren
Wouldn't it be nice
It's too cold here
We could take the boat
Loaded with our gear
Rent a shack with pontoon
On the Hawkesbury

Note to self
Must but lottery ticket
Only need another million

Definitely a first-world problem
Stop waiting
This is it!

And Lazy Daisy Chain Days were just fine

The Ceremony

Found deep in a Christmas stocking
About Grade Four
Reflected in the mirror
It did the job over and over without complaint
It had just the right grip
Yellow plastic handle
Translucent bristles
Through short brown locks
A grooming companion

Serving you well through those turbulent teens
And sun bleached tresses
Carted through college
Packed up and relocated
So many addresses
Finally in a place of your own

It was there on your Wedding Day
At Births
Christenings
Marriages
Funerals
Sometimes used by a little hand
On those dogs it was certainly banned

It became a seasoned traveller
Planes trains automobiles
Too many cities
Countless country roads
Small villages

Over the decades
The pressure was too much
Reluctantly
Gradually
It discarded bristles
Uncompromising service slowly diminished

'How could you?
You can't just trash it'
Without ceremony
In some random council wheelie bin
Destined for hard fill
Earths slow compression

Carefully centred on a beautiful white plate
We take a few photos reminiscing about its adventure
Our symbolic farewell gesture

Such a trusty little hairbrush
Yet with no appetite for hoarding we bin it
A replacement found
Although nothing can compare
But it matters not with so little hair

The Butterfly

I hadn't prayed in years
It happened on that island
The Jewell of India
Minibus meanderings
Hours of it
Traffic so slow one could scream
'Calm down'
Rattles in my head

Hail Mary
Who was that woman
She must have been something to deserve a hail
Full of grace
I wish that were me presently
The lord is with you
She managed upwards with tenderness
Blessed are you amongst women
Surrounded by girlfriends who loved her
Blessed is the fruit of your womb
How can I forget
She gave birth to a man that for thousands of years has inspired billions
Holy Mary
She was the Mother of a God
Pray for us sinners
I need all the help I can get
Now and at the hour of our death
Especially on these roads with our driver who is nodding off
Amen

Flippancy ignored
Waves of peace float over and through me in ways that cannot
be explained
Perhaps it was the sun streaming through
Maybe those hypnotic tea plantations
Or that Holy Spirit finally showering me forty years post-
Confirmation

Later I learnt of my Mother's passing during my hour of
prayer
They said it was a blessing

In the form of a beautiful white Sri Lankan butterfly I felt her
again
Fluttering to rest on my hand
I watch patiently for just a few seconds
And it meant the world to me

Although absent he was convinced it was a cabbage moth

Fade Away

We gazed upward quite amazed
Swaying gently in the breeze
'Is that mottled leopard skin?'
Stretched taught against the blistering sun
Faded to milky yellow
So beautiful in its own repurposed way
Go figure
An old mattress protector with street cred
So imperfectly perfect
Yet delightfully disturbing

Time on My Hands

Little treasures
Accomplished prehensile
Having lived a life of involuntary servitude
That most richest source of tactile feedback

Obeying the mind
Grasping concepts not only objects
Doing just what they're told
Dexterous and delicate
Adequate yet priceless
A bit wrinkled though cleansed

I have another two precious hands
My first son
Plaster set
Embedded with string
Little

My youngest son
Bright red
Stamped and framed
Just as little

On that wall together
Helped by my hands

Another touching sentiment

Nana's Gift

It is my last link
A baby card
Handwritten to me
From a woman I hardly knew
From a Nana I so loved
As all kids do

Iced Vovo and lemonade
A garden full of gladioli
Every Sunday after Mass
All dressed in white
Lace mantilla discarded

They would confide
We would play
Oblivious to her struggle

Too young to see
Through her veiled smile
Domestic violence so carefully concealed

Chemical Fragility

I love that feeling
When totally inspired
Absorbed in the moment
Watching and seeing
Listening and hearing

The way it tingles around then moves through your heart
Involuntarily it radiates
To your throat
Face eyes and lips
A swallow
A smile
A tear

Exquisite chemistry
I used to suppress that feeling
Sometimes I still do

I don't know why

I Don't Buy It

Third shelf up
They beckon
I resist
They beckon again
Just one…I promise

I used to tear at the packet with my teeth
Slowly does it
Savour the moment
Out come the scissors
Look graceful
One only…I promise

I prefer Tim Tams and Fruchocs
Or Violet Crumble
You can't go pass a box of Roses or Favourites
Better still Quality Street or affordable Black Magic
Ferrero Rocher are delicious
Lindt are nice too
But nothing beats Haigh's

Ah…back in the day
I did like Bountys
Mars bars were the best
So were Cherry Ripe
And don't forget Bertie Beatles
Remember Polly Waffles
And Wagon Wheels
And Rocky Road
And Scorched Almonds
And Jaffa's at the Saturday matinée
And home-made chocolate crackles at parties
And there is definitely nothing wrong
With just a plain block of Cadbury chocolate or Fruit & Nut

My addiction passes
I have high cholesterol
They still beckon
But from a safer distance

I don't buy chocolates any more
Gifts are welcome

Where Will It End

I write fluidly
Sometimes laboriously
Languishing on just the right expression
Pausing to grasp meaning
Transforming thought to word

I once used scraps of paper
Some even found their way into my Scrap Book
Hidden away from critics
In that bottom drawer

Who invented 'Scrap'
It sounds like trash
It rhymes with crap
How can it be the incomplete works of me
Mere pieces of scrap in a Scrap Book

And where does it end?
The funeral held
The sad clean out one room at a time
Papers in one pile clothes in another
Jewellery toiletries cookbooks CDs
Underwhelming

Scraps are now 'Notes'
My phone so smart so convenient so backed-up in a cloud
So much nicer than scrap
A 'Note' end is different
Electronic waste recycling
To that depot where old hard drives and screens are sorted
Plastic
Wire
Copper
Help save the planet

Piles of PCs TVs VCRs microwaves fridges
All worth money
Eventually de-manufactured
Stripped and conveyed
Packaged and shipped
Sold and reused
My words
Mere binary code lost in a mountain of hardware and cloud

I think I prefer scrap
Perhaps I should publish
But where will it end?

The Proximity of Things

Those slender grasses covered in dainty purple flowers have jumped our border
Quite disobedient at first glance
But it's just their own relentless path-encroaching survival march

Light years away our sun streams ultraviolet rays to infiltrate my shoulders at this early hour
I reach for a sarong
It's a hot one

Coffee half-finished stands sentinel as honeyeaters battle for ringside seats
A little water world amongst the natives
I wonder about bird bath pecking protocol
Deep in birdsong and words my hours float away

Oblivious to it all they sleep on
Each in dream time
From a night of wine

I don't have it all figured out
And never will
We can leave it there
But we really can't
Wisdom is so close to all of us
Yet it slips on past

It's easier to stay here
Close to things
Than to say the things we really mean

Another note to self
Start interfering in things

No Time to Waste

Before I was born
I cannot recall a thing

Not frightening
Not peaceful
Just a non-existence

Perhaps death is the same
Not heaven
Not hell

So open your eyes now
It's not such a waste
Of that retina space

Cubanism

It was a lovely quiet event
Familiar friends coming together once again
Exchanging festive happenings
Watching the kids-session fireworks fizzers and old flares
Reflecting on that ghostly bay

Decades past those boozy screamers
Stilettos balloons and streamers

A massive woolly bush sculptured snapper stares back at us
Oblivious to our frivolity
Ignoring fished-out fragility

Champagne stands in line
Wearing ice-pack stoles
Perched safely in their buckets
We also stand in line
Watching our bubbles rise through slender crystal
Chilled to the bone wondering when summer will start

Glasses charged
Ten nine eight seven
We turn our backs
As a burst of colour lights the blackness
Greenwich Mean Time smirks with sadistic non-synchronistic glee

Our host now alone for the toast seeks solace
That cigar slips out cautiously
His retirement gift waiting so patiently
Guilty of neglect we turn back and raise our glasses
Another round of hugs and kisses

Meanwhile the scent hits home
In muffled whispers all hell breaks loose
We shuffle away pretending not to eavesdrop
Something about '…stop it'
then '…don't f*<#'g break it'
Not quite war and peace
It slithers back to pocket
Scheming its next move

What the heck
What about the boat deck

The Grumball

What makes someone take six rum balls
Instead of one
A fist full
In the other hand a chocolate too
Pinkie held just so

We all glare
Then look elsewhere
We no longer care
And no one comments

Leaving few for others
Some blame his brothers
No one blames the mother
Nor his toughened father

Perhaps just too delicious
Perhaps a yuletide appetite

Plate replenished
He does it again
No one comments

Yet another note to self
Make more next year

Mother and Son

I see him now
Adorable
Not yet at school
Blond blue-eyed innocence
Choosing carefully amongst so many
A tiny purple flower in hand
'…because you are lovely'

Discovered hard-pressed
Twenty years later
Pure beauty in word and gesture

We smile again

Finding Fontaine

Love love
Sweetest of harmonies
May you always recognise her face
Savour his delights
Feel her whisper
Breathe his fragrance
All the rest is nothing

What Now

Who Are These People

They hang on every word he says
Knowing minds
Watching him
Watching me listen to him
He leaves us
My transient guardian angels stay a short while
Pathology underway
I wait

The Coming Out

At the touch of love everyone becomes a poet
Plato at his best
At the touch of sickness I become a poet
Not quite at my best

Three Months Later

First floor up
Check-in was pleasant enough
We laugh about a coincidence
'It's a nice name' I say

Entering was a shock as I pondered book titles
Logistics of Modern Medicine
Dollar Forced Efficacy
Triage Rack and Stack

In both directions
Yet to be partitioned
Beds stretch out into the distance
Abandoned at 15
Left to fidget
Ignoring the blue gown
I try my demure-but-definitely-not-at-home look

Words float in space
I force myself to concentrate
A touching short story about death and moving on
Scanning the room
Not quite 'Dream Stuff' from this angle

It is all very interesting
Some are eager even compliant
Gowned up they pop straight into bed
Whisking the curtain open
Obviously not their first time

'Walk forward'
I shuffle
'Walk forward'
Oh…I get it
Height taken
'On the scales'
She frowns
Mumbling about BMI being under
'How old are you'
Shaking her head

Back to the book
What now
Curtains drawn
Politely persuaded to disrobe
How is anyone supposed to tie this thing

I lie
Hiding behind the crisp blue
Cold
My stomach complains
She throws them open
How dare anyone have privacy
She brings me a warm blanket
I love this nurse

Snuggling deep
Solitude regained
Wheeling me away
Smiling faces
Hair net so I don't look better than the rest
Another warm blanket
I love these orderlies

Now three blankets deep
Hiding
'You look healthy'
I'm having a lazy afternoon
He's going to the cricket
How quaint
I love my anaesthetist

'I'm all good Doctor'
'Let's see about that'
Wheeled away once again
Tension mounts
Why does he avoid eye contact

Forced walk into theatre
My gown gets caught
All grace gone

An hour later
Listening to them whisper
'BMI could have been wrong'
Water and sandwich coffee and cake
That nurse can't do a thing wrong

My husband arrives
Unshaven
I smile
Curtains open
Waiting
Waiting

'Good news all clear'
I love my doctor

Roads Too Travelled

I Want to be a Wallaby

I want to be a wallaby
And live on Wallaby Creek Road
It's next to Sandy Hollow Creek
Near those Hunter Valley vines
But coal trucks rumble
Trains haul on
Overburden conveyors and power poles confuse my path
Wildlife injury signs are here and there
Grandma said we should have moved
To Spring Gully ten moons ago
I want to be a wallaby
…but I'm roadkill

I See the Light

Billions of stars stud my perfect night sky
Illuminating a vast desert
Bilby scurry
Quokkas forage
Sweet peace
Like no other a distant light escapes the horizon
All I want to do is hop like a kangaroo
…you guessed it I'm roadkill

Forty in the Shade

Blinding white sand scorches me
Ocean and sky merge in the distance
I meander through scrub
Across rocky limestone
And a litany of haphazard tracks
What a pain
I cry in vain
For heaven's sake
No longer a snake
…I'm flattened roadkill

You're Kidding Me

Sad but true
Staring out the window
In disbelief
We frown at each other
Speechless
It's a sad thing
Quite disturbing
Poor lost soul
A little spiky bundle
Once an echidna
Now it's just roadkill

I'm Flying Along

Road stretched out for miles
Tail wind and
Heading home
Lines look like dots
I smile
Free as a bird
Oh no
Badged
Nissan or Toyota
Who can tell
Slammed into my chest
All I wanted was my nest
…and now look at me I'm roadkill

It Was the Winter

Of my discontent
Now where did I read that
Seven long months
Bitter wind
Icy cold
Rain and hail
Tedious
Stuck inside
Like a bad scent cabin fever hovers
At last
Sunshine
Sweet heat
Delicious on my skin
Heating deep to the bone
Eyes closed
I see orange then red with each eyelid squeeze
Aahh
I wake
Oh oh
What's this
Surrounded by gizzard
No longer a sleepy lizard
…I can't believe I'm roadkill

Brecon Beacon

I was a chosen one
Pure they said
Fit for a national park
Released into the wild
Rolling hills and rich pasture
As far as the eye can see
With companions to choose
Fresh air
Fence free
Sweet harmony
What more could one want
I was the perfect pony
Now I am mere roadkill

Where Devils Venture

Locked in this cell
Day after dreary day
At their beck and call
I am innocent
Three meals a day will never compensate
Finally I make parole
Tagged to track my whereabouts
Avoid people my mantra
Deep into the wilderness I venture
Always on the level
I was a Tasmanian Devil
…but of course now I'm roadkill

It's a Sad Thing

Maybe it's the way I look
People love to hate me
I haven't done a thing wrong
Our kind have been here for decades
Everyone's a blow-in
Unless you're fifth generation
Now they worry
As we head south
In search of a safe place to call home
What is it with this mob
Not in my backyard their cry
I'm used to it
I just smirk and answer back
They are repulsed
Battered about
Kicked around
Frozen out
What I would give for one last goad
Even though I'm a sad cane toad
…as you can probably guess I'm roadkill

Sweet Infant

My mother died when I was so young
They looked after me a while
Five tiny meals a day
They sent me on my way
What was I thinking
Dumb and numb
I was a numbat
…now I'm even dumber roadkill

Everyone Loved Jack

His circling madness
Hilarious
Chicken scaring
Dog-shaking antics
We all hear the bang
A loud yelp
The driver is shaking
Men stare in disbelief
Women hide
Gut wrenching
It was quick
So random
We discuss Eddie
She mentions Lady
Life and laughter
Death and destruction
All part of the package
…and now he's roadkill
It's not so funny any more

Not the Way to Go

Road accident signage so Australian style
Mainly outback
Quite cryptic
Flat plastic-coated metal sticks along the way
Rising from roadside gravel
Stark and sombre
Red marks an injury
Black for fatality
A perforated cross replaces a reflector
Some alone
Some together
One black one red
Two or three black
Sometimes a whole family
Gone
Gender irrelevant
Age unknown
I wonder about stick-death bureaucracy
Rights of refusal
Who instigates and installs
What cost and maintenance
Some repudiate a mere marker
Too irreverent perhaps
I saw a hockey stick
Then a bicycle
Two crossed fishing rods
A scarecrow once
Even a small polished engine truck
Teddy bear and flowers
Old dusty swag

Individualised
Dignified
Regardless of those poor lost souls
We are all reminded
'Drowsy Drivers Die'
Yet so might the innocent nearby

A Final Word

My Little Universe

It's hot
One of those must-find-shade days

I'm stretched out staring up at canvas
Interstellar like tiny dust particles
Float erratically on a sun beam shining my way
A marvellous microcosm

Halting for no one earth speeds away
That sun continues on
My universal illusion disappears
I close my eyes
Content yet not deluded
It's still out there

About the Author

Donna Edwards is a writer and world traveller. Foremost a poet at heart, she prefers to write for leisure, including personalised poems and short stories for her family. She has also written a screenplay and a children's story, which remain hidden in her scrapbook. Her poems have been used in selected advanced English classes. When she is not travelling for inspiration, Donna lives in Adelaide and Marion Bay with her family.

www.ingramcontent.com/pod-product-compliance
Lightning Source LLC
Chambersburg PA
CBHW070914080526
44589CB00013B/1291